Science Around the House

Simple Projects Using Household Recyclables

Roz Fulcher

Dover Publications, Inc.
Mineola, New York

Bibliographical Note

Science Around the House: Simple Projects Using Household Recyclables
is a new work, first published by Dover Publications, Inc., in 2010.

International Standard Book Number
ISBN-13: 978-0-486-47645-2
ISBN-10: 0-486-47645-6

Manufactured in the United States by Courier Corporation
47645601
www.doverpublications.com

NOTE

Need something to do on a rainy day—or even on a sunny day? Take a look around your house for string, plastic milk jugs, butter containers, empty jars, and other items that would normally be thrown away and recycle them as you create 57 fun science projects. Learn how to "bend" water, make your own bouncy ball, clone a plant, and change the color of a flower. Also included are some tasty activities like ice cream making and cooking baked Alaska to learn about insulation! On a nice day you can go outside and collect grasshoppers and crickets for a bug study, go on a rock scavenger hunt, and make a wormery. These projects make learning about science fun!

Before starting any of these projects, please let an adult know so they can supervise. Many of the projects in this book require help from an adult. This is indicated by a caution symbol $\triangledown\!\!\!\!!$ in either the top left, or top right corner of the page.

Acid Rain

Every type of material will erode from the effects of the climate, but acid rain can make this happen much quicker.

Power stations, factories and cars all burn fuels, which produce polluting gases. Some of these gases react with tiny droplets of water in clouds to form sulphuric and nitric acids. The rain from these clouds fall as weak acid. This is **acid rain**.

Chalk is made of calcium, the same as in limestone and marble. Vinegar and lemon juice are forms of acid. You can see how acid rain affects rocks and buildings over hundreds of years.

WATER

LEMON JUICE

VINEGAR

You will need:

3 deli containers

vinegar   water

lemon juice   chalk

Fill each container 1/2 full with vinegar, water and lemon juice. Put a piece of chalk in each cup making sure it is in the liquid. Observe your cups for the next several days. What happened?

A"MAZE"ing Plant!

You will need:

card stock

runner bean

cup of dirt

shoe box

scissors

water

1 Cut a large window in one end of the shoe box and card stock.

2 Soak your bean in water for 24 hours and then plant it in a container of soil (not too deep).

3 Fit a piece of card stock in the box and place the container of soil underneath it, away from the window you made in the card stock.

4 Put the lid on the shoe box and place in a warm, bright area.

All green plants need light to grow. **Phototropism** is the process where plants grow toward their light source.

5

ter your seed regularly en soil gets dry. As your nt grows, add another ndow" card. Watch your nt find its way through maze!

The plant grows toward the sunlight even though the card stock pieces are in the way.

Bending Water

Static electricity has amazing power to attract things - even running water!

Static electricity is the build up of electrical charges on the surface of an object or material. It's usually created when things are pulled apart or rubbed together causing (+) charges to collect on one material and (-) charges on the other surface.

Opposite charges attract each other. The neutral water is attracted to the charged balloon and moves towards it.

Rub wool sweater with latex balloon or stroke hair at least 10 times with a comb. Turn on the tap so a narrow stream of water is flowing. Move the balloon or comb close to the water (but not in it). Watch the stream bend toward your comb/balloon.

*This experiment works best on a dry day.

Bouncy Ball

White glue and cornstarch are both **polymers** (long-chained molecules). Borax causes cross-links to develop between the two polymers, which makes the mixture stiff.

Add more water to the borax solution and instead of bouncy balls you can make play putty.

Container #1: Add 1 teaspoon of borax to 2 tablespoons of warm water. Stir to dissolve.
Container #2: Mix 1 tablespoon of glue with 2 teaspoons of cornstarch.

Add 1 teaspoon of borax mixture (container #1) to the glue/cornstarch mixture (container #2). Stir well. The mixture will become stiff. Tip it out of the container and knead into a ball. You've made a bouncy ball!

You will need:

Borax (found in the laundry aisle)

warm water

yogurt cups #1 #2

teaspoon and tablespoon

spoon

white glue

Bug Study

What's the difference between a cricket and a grasshopper?

Grasshoppers...
-are diurnal (active in the day).
-are vividly green in color to fit in well in their grassy habitat.
-call to other grasshoppers but also use keen sight to find them.
-have brightly colored underwings that they flash when they fly.
-have short antennae.
-have ears that are located in their abdomen.

lamp for warmth

netting fabric -

clear plastic box or fish tank -

- lettuce, cabbage, or grass, replaced daily

potting soil/dirt

Grasshopper habitat:

short plastic cup filled with damp sand (for laying eggs)

 toilet roll and twigs for climbing

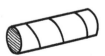 bran or wheat germ

Crickets...
- are nocturnal (active at night).
- are dark in color (pale green to brown) to blend in the shadows at night.
- chirp at night to communicate with other crickets.
- do not fly.
- have long antennae.
- have ears in their legs (look for a white dot near the bend of each leg).

Grasshopper

Cricket

hose or cloth secured with rubber band

large glass jar

Cricket habitat:

dry pet food, fish flakes, wheat germ or bran.

wet cotton ball in plastic lid

egg carton pieces for hiding places

coarse grass or shredded newspaper

Cloning Plants

Cloning a plant means you are making a plant that is identical to another. Almost any part of the plant (roots, stems, leaves) can be used for reproduction.

The 2 major functions of **roots** are 1) absorption of water 2) anchoring the plant in the ground.

You will need:

scissors

clear jar of water

To grow a new plant, have an adult help you snip a long piece of plant and place it in a clear jar full of tap water. This way you can observe the root growth. Be sure leaves aren't sitting in the water or they will rot. Keep checking daily for root buds. After a couple of weeks the roots will become thick and strong (the first root that comes from a plant is called a **radical**). At this point you can leave your plant growing in the water or plant in soil.

Pothos, (or any viney plant) works great for this project.

Crayon Melts

You will need:
crayon bits
tin cans
ice tray or candy mold

Wax can change from a solid to a liquid when heated. It will become a solid again when it cools.

3. Place tin cans in a pan of shallow water and have an adult helper melt crayons on medium low heat.

2. Place crayon bits into tin cans

1. Remove paper from crayons and break into small bits.

4. Have an adult also help pour hot wax into the ice tray or candy molds. Leave to cool for 20 minutes.

5. Voila! New crayons.

Didgeridoos & Kazoos

Create sound waves using household cardboard tubing.

Sound is a type of energy made by vibrations.

-A **kazoo** is an instrument that makes the sound of your humming louder when the wax paper buzzes and vibrates.

Kazoo:

wax paper

rubber band

Have an adult poke 2 holes in your tube.

- A **didgeridoo** is a long wind instrument used by the Aborigines of Australia. Make your own with a wrapping paper tube. Make motorboat sounds into your didgeridoo.

Eating Iron

blender

hot tap water

The chemical symbol for iron is **Fe**. Iron aids in the formation of red blood cells and they help to transport oxygen through your system.

Pour 1 cup of cereal into a blender with 2 cups of hot tap water. Blend until you have a very fine, soupy mixture. Pour into a plastic storage container. Tape a magnet to the eraser end of a pencil. Stir your mixture for 10 minutes with the magnet. Wipe the magnet on a coffee filter.

Magnets attract iron. Metallic iron is added to fortified cereal. The process of pulling the iron from the cereal is called **recovery**.

iron fortified cereal

super strong magnet

measuring cup

pencil

plastic storage bag

tape

coffee filter

Build a Battery

Have an adult help you strip the ends of both lengths of insulated copper wire. Mix a cup of water with 2 tablespoons of salt. Trace your penny on the paper towel and tin foil to create 10 disks of each (if you use more than 10 pennies just make sure to make equal amounts of paper/foil disks). Cut paper a little larger than outline and the foil the same size as outline. Take your paper towel disks and soak them in the salt water solution.

The coins and foil react with the salt water to create **electricity**.This flows along the wires.

The pennies act as the **electrodes** and the salt water serves as the **electrolyte** in this single cell battery.

You will need:

10 - 15 pennies (copper coins)

2 tablespoons salt

cup of water

2 lengths of insulated copper wire

To build your battery, take your copper wire and tape it to a foil disk (this is the base of your battery). Set it wire side down and place a paper disk on top, followed by a penny. Continue to build - foil, paper, penny - until you have completed the pile. Tape your second length of copper wire to the last penny you use. Touch the two free ends of the wire together to test your battery. In a dark room, you should see a spark!

This simple battery is a **voltaic pile**. "Voltaic" is a set of individual Galvanic cells placed in a series which was invented by Alessandro Volta in the 1800s.

penny

paper

foil

scissors

tweezers

tape

tin foil

paper towel

Egg Arch

Discover how strong even the arch of an egg can be.

An **arch** is a curved structure that supports or strengthens a building.

Arches are strong because they use **horizontal** and **vertical** forces to support the pressure of heavy loads.

cut -

scissors

masking tape

books

Wrap masking tape around the center of each egg and have an adult help you pierce and cut your eggs in half. Use the wider end of the eggs for your arches. Pour the egg liquid in a cup and use for cooking. Place the egg arches on a table and gently place one book at a time on top of the eggs. Predict how many books you think the egg shells can support.

((Egg Spinning))

Set a raw egg on a plate and spin the egg. Lightly touch it with your finger and as soon as it stops, pull your finger away. Next, repeat the experiment with a hard-boiled egg. How did the two eggs behave?

When I stopped the raw egg from spinning, it didn't actually stop because the contents (yolk and whites) were still spinning. The hard-boiled egg stopped spinning because its contents were solid.

raw egg

hard-boiled egg

Inertia is the principle that an object will keep moving at a constant speed and direction unless something acts to change it.

Butterfly Feeder

Butterflies enjoy a liquid diet from fruit trees and flower nectars. Attract them to your garden with homemade nectar. Observe and document the different species that visit.

Sugar nectar recipe:
Mix 9 parts water to 1 part sugar (teaspoons work well for this project.) Bring to a boil in the microwave until sugar has dissolved.

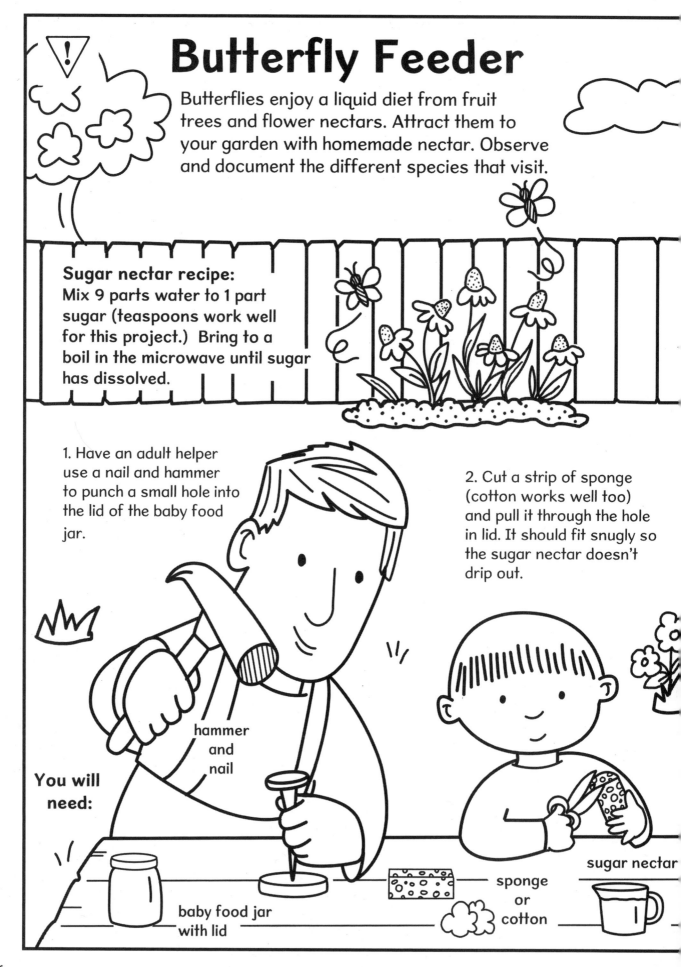

1. Have an adult helper use a nail and hammer to punch a small hole into the lid of the baby food jar.

2. Cut a strip of sponge (cotton works well too) and pull it through the hole in lid. It should fit snugly so the sugar nectar doesn't drip out.

hammer and nail

You will need:

baby food jar with lid

sponge or cotton

sugar nectar

Butterflies have a tubular tongue called a **probiscus** that is used like a drinking straw to suck nectar and other liquids.

We also enjoy over ripe fruit. Hang a 1/2 gallon ice-cream lid from a tree filled with bananas, oranges or watermelon slices.

3. Tie a piece of string around the "mouth" of the baby food jar. Cut 2 lengths of string about 30 inches long and attach each end to the string around the jar (this will create 2 loops). Use one more length of string to tie the loops together for hanging. Turn your jar upside down and make sure it hangs steadily.

4. Decorate your jar with fake flowers or colorful stickers. This will help attract your butterflies.

5. Fill your jar with the sugar nectar and attach the lid tightly. Turn upside down and hang on a tree branch.

string

stickers and fake flowers

glue stick

17

Eggshell Planters

Wash eggshells with warm, soapy water and decorate with funny faces. Place egg shells in an egg carton and spoon soil carefully into the shells. Press grass seeds into the soil gently and dampen with water. Place near a sunny window and water when soil gets dry.

Plants use energy from the sun to change carbon dioxide and water into starches and sugars. This process is called **photosynthesis**.

Nutrients in the soil are dissolved in water and absorbed through the plant's roots.

water

soil

markers

left over eggshells
from cooking/baking

grass seeds

Fake Snot

Have an adult helper heat water until it boils. Turn the heat off and add a tiny drop of food coloring to the water. Sprinkle in the unflavored gelatin and stir in with a fork. Add enough corn syrup to make 1 cup of thick mixture. With your fork, lift out the long strands of goo.

You will need:

fork

3 packets gelatin

green food coloring

1/2 cup of water

corn syrup

Mucus is mainly made out of sugars and proteins. That is what we used to make the fake mucus, just different proteins and sugars.

The long strands of goo are **proteins**. The protein in mucus is what makes it sticky and stretchy.

Fall Forecast

Do this project to see the hidden color in leaves that will appear in the Fall.

Tear the leaves into tiny bits and place them in a plastic container (use a separate container for each type of leaf you use). Add just enough rubbing alcohol to cover them. Cover the container with plastic wrap to prevent evaporation and place it in a shallow dish of hot tap water. While your mixture turns green (takes about 30 minutes), cut your coffee filter into a 1/2 inch strip and tape to a pencil. Rest the pencil along the container's rim. Make sure the paper strip is touching the mixture. Observe the different pigments that the mixture separates into.

Leaves contain different **pigments** which give them their color. The most common is **chlorophyll** (green) but there are also **cartenoids** (yellow, orange) and **anthocyanins**(red).

The act of separating the components of a mixture is called **chromotography.**

Green tree leaves

- pencil

- plastic container

rubbing alcohol

plastic wrap

scissors

shallow dish with hot tap water

tape

coffee filter

20

Magnet Fishing Game

- Make fish shapes with scrap construction paper and attach a steel paper clip.

The first magnets were made out of black rock called **Lodestones.** Modern magnets are made out of steel.

Magnets attract metal. This is called **Magnetic Force.**

- Decorate a cardboard box to look like an underwater scene.

Try a shoe box.

- Tie string to a long stick.
Tape a magnet to the end of string to make your fishing pole.

Edible Insulation

Baked Alaska:

Egg whites from 3 eggs
1/4 tsp cream of tartar
1/4 tsp salt
1/2 tsp vanilla extract
big cookies
ice cream
1 cup of sugar

Have an adult helper preheat oven at 500 degrees. Put egg whites, cream of tartar, salt and vanilla extract in a bowl and whisk with a mixer until stiff peaks form. Slowly add sugar a tablespoon at a time to the mixture while continuing to whisk.

Place some cookies on your baking pan, leaving room between them. (The cookies should be chilled in the freezer before cooking.) Place a small scoop of ice cream on each cookie making sure that the ice cream doesn't spill over the edges. Spoon the meringue mixture (whisked egg whites) over the ice cream and the cookie. All the ice cream must be covered completely by the meringue. Have an adult place the cookie sheet in the oven and bake for 5 minutes or until golden brown. Eat immediately and enjoy!

Air and carbon dioxide are trapped in the beaten egg. They act as an **insulator**.

mixer

bowl

cookie sheet

cream of tartar

spoon

sugar

eggs

vanilla extract

measuring tools

cookies

22

oven

The **meringue** (egg whites) protects the ice cream from the heat of the oven.

lation
ws the
vement
ot or cold.

ice cream

23

Thirsty Flowers

Fill 3 bottles with water and add a few drops of different food coloring to each. Take 3 white flowers and trim the stems. Place a flower in each bottle and leave overnight. The petals have changed into the color of the water they are drinking.

Plants need water to stay alive. Water moves through the plant in tiny tubes called **capillaries**. Water travels up the stem and spreads to all parts of the plant including the petals.

3 white flowers
(carnations work great)

You will need:

food coloring

scissors

3 water bottles

Gummy Science

Gummy candies are made with glucose, starch and gelatin. The water can be absorbed but the starch and gelatin cannot. So the water swells the gummy- a lot like a sponge.

You will need:

ruler

gummy candies &
plastic container filled with water

Choose a gummy candy and measure its length and width (or trace around the gummy). Record your measurements. Place your gummy in a container of tap water. After 24 hours, carefully remove your gummy and place it on a paper towel. Measure your gummy and compare the difference in size.

For the Birds

gallon jug

Birds love moving water. Have an adult help you cut the top off of a gallon jug and fill with water. Pierce a tiny hole in the bottom to allow water to drip through. Hang above a birdbath.

To build a birdbath, take a plant saucer and rest it on an inverted terra-cotta pot. Take rocks and place inside the saucer. This will keep the saucer in place and also give birds a place to rest. Fill with water and replace regularly to keep the bath area clean.

Plant saucer

pot

The scientific study of birds is called **Ornithology**. Bird study includes: **classification, evolution, body structure, habits, song, flight** and **breeding behavior**. Winter feeding gives you an excellent opportunity to observe and study wild birds in your very own backyard. They will be attracted to your garden if you provide food, shelter and water.

Towards spring, birds will be looking for material to build nests. Take an onion or orange mesh bag and fill with bits of string, yarn, cotton, strips of fabric and twigs. Hang from a fence post.

Tie a long string to pinecones and corn husks. Slather peanut butter over pinecones and corn husks. Roll in bird seed and hang from trees. Your birds will love dining on this treat.

onion or orange mesh bag

nesting material

peanut butter

bird seed

string

corn husk

pinecones

Ice Melting Race

Solar Energy is light and heat that comes from the sun. When a color absorbs light, it turns the light into **thermal energy** (heat). The more light a color absorbs, the more thermal energy it produces. Black absorbs the most light and white reflects it. Since there are **gradients** of color, you will see gradients of absorption.

white

black

violet

yellow

blue

orange

Choose a warm, sunny day and lay 6 sheets of colored construction paper outside (black and white should be included in this experiment). Place an ice cube on each card. Ready, set, go! Observe which ice cubes melt the fastest and slowest.

Ice Cream in a Bag

Combine sugar, vanilla and half & half in the small bag. Seal bag. Mix ice and rock salt in the large bag. Place the small bag into the the large one and seal tightly. Now shake, shake, shake! Keep shaking for 5 minutes. Take the small bag out of the large one and eat the ice cream straight from the bag.
Enjoy!

Ice cream is a **colloid** which is a chemical mixture where 2 substances are suspended within each other but don't bond.

Salt lowers the **freezing point** of water which causes the ice to melt at a lower temperature. The lower freezing point provides the temperature difference needed to transfer heat between the ingredients and melting ice.

1/2 cup

half & half

1 pint and 1 gallon storage bag

1 tablespoon sugar

vanilla extract

rock salt

1/2 cup

ice

Invisible Ink

Squeeze lemon juice into a saucer, add a few drops of water and mix together with a spoon. Use a cotton swab or paintbrush to write a message on a piece of paper. When it dries, the writing will be invisible. Heat the paper by holding it written side down near a light bulb to reveal the secret message!

Top Secret

The lemon juice has compounds of carbon. When you heat them, the **carbon compounds** break down and turn brown.

You will need:

paintbrush

paper

cotton swab

spoon

saucer

lemons

light bulb

Picture Magic

1. Draw a fish on an index card and color it red. Draw a black eye.

2. On another card, draw the outline (black) of a fish bowl that your fish will fit inside.

3. Sit in a well lit area and stare at your red fish for 20 seconds, focusing on the eye. Next, quickly stare at your fish bowl card. What do you see? What color is it?

Create different magical pictures and store them in a plastic container. Draw a lion on one card and an outline of a cage on another, for example. Color the lion red, blue, or green.

The special effect you see is an **afterimage** which means the image stays with you even after you have stopped looking at it.

blank index cards

plastic container

red, blue, green, and black crayons or markers

The back of your eyes are lined with light-sensitive cells called **cones**. Cones have three color receptors that are most sensitive to red, green and blue. When you stared at the red fish for a long time the receptor got tired and your eyes used the blue and green cones that were stronger. This is why your fish changed color in the **afterimage**.

Indoor Composting

Compost is a dark earthy material made up of decomposing material.

Composting works very much like a forest ecosyst

1. Have an adult cut off the bottom 1/4 of a soda bottle. This will be your "lid."

2. Place the panty hose scrap over t spout and secure it with a rubber ba This will be for drainage.

You will need:

panty hose scrap

rubber band

cut -

soda bottle

plastic deli tub

water

scissors

Decomposers break down dead organisms into nutrients. As these organisms "rot," the nutrients return to the soil.

This new soil is loaded with nitrogen, phosphorous and potassium. Your compost should be ready in a month to use in your house plants or garden.

3. Place the bottle upside down in a deli container and fill with composting material. Layer browns, greens, dirt and shredded paper.

4. Add water and stir until everything is as damp as a sponge. Add your lid made from the bottom of the soda bottle.
Stir weekly. You can reuse the water that collects into the deli container.

owns"

"greens"

Tip: Crush egg shells and chop vegetable scraps before adding to compost to help speed up the "rotting."

Lava Lamp

Make a Sunset

Fill a glass jar with cold water and add a splash of milk. In a darkened room, shine a flashlight on the side of the jar. What color do you see?

The milk represents the Earth's **atmosphere,** which is made of invisible gases and tiny particles of dust. The sky color changes because the atmosphere spreads the light according to the position of the sun. When the sun is low (sunset and sunrise) it passes through more air than other parts of the day. Only orange and red light gets through.

You will need:

milk

jar of water

spoon

flashlight

Ocean In A Bottle

Bottle waves are like ocean waves. Ocean waves get their energy from wind. Higher waves need more energy.

plastic bottle

oil

water

vegetable oil

water

funnel

food coloring

Fill your bottle 3/4 full with water and add blue food coloring to make your ocean. Add tiny shells or glitter if you like. Fill the rest of the bottle with oil, using a funnel. Screw on cap tightly and turn your bottle on its side. Move your bottle back and forth to make waves.

Water is **denser** (heavier) than oil so it sinks to the bottom.

Purifying Water

The sun warms the water, causing it to change from a liquid to a gas (**water vapor**). The vapor rises and **condenses** to form water on the plastic wrap. It runs down toward the rock and drips back into the cup. This is called the **hydrologic cycle** (water cycle).

To make "polluted water," fill a large bowl with water about 1/4 full. Add a couple of spoons of salt and a few drops of food coloring. Stir. Next, place an empty plastic container in the middle of the bowl. Cover the bowl loosely with plastic wrap. Place a marble or rock in the center of the wrap, making sure it's directly over the cup (you want the wrap to dip towards the cup). Make sure there is a seal around the lip of the bowl and the wrap. You can secure it with a rubber band. Leave it in the sun for several hours to purify.

plastic wrap

spoon

plastic container

salt

food coloring

rocks or marbles

water

Kaleidoscope

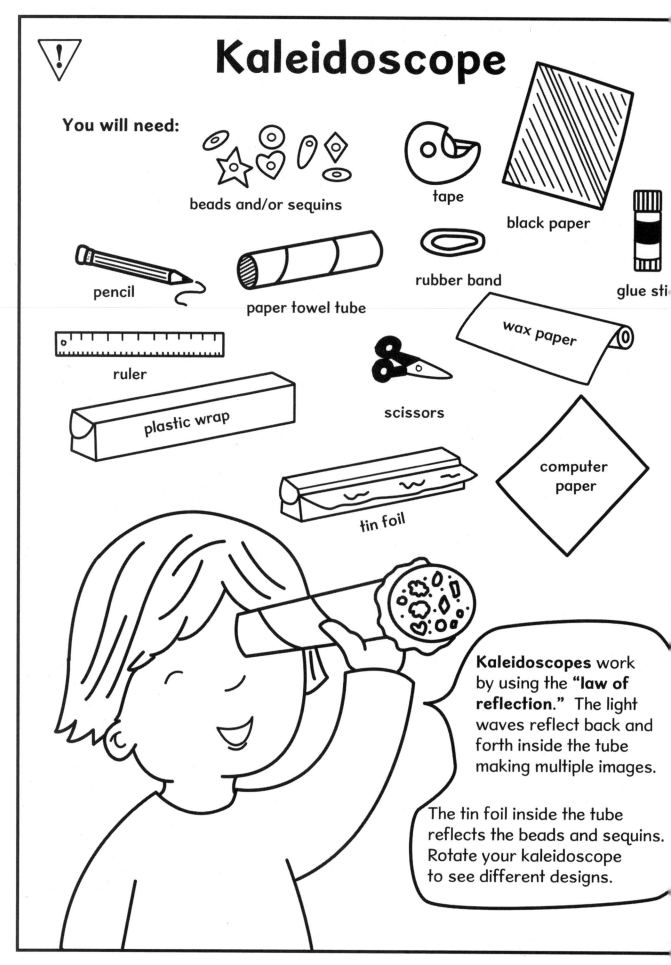

You will need:

beads and/or sequins

tape

black paper

glue stick

pencil

paper towel tube

rubber band

ruler

wax paper

plastic wrap

scissors

computer paper

tin foil

Kaleidoscopes work by using the **"law of reflection."** The light waves reflect back and forth inside the tube making multiple images.

The tin foil inside the tube reflects the beads and sequins. Rotate your kaleidoscope to see different designs.

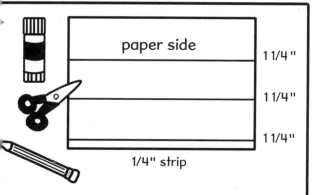

paper side

1 1/4 "

1 1/4 "

1 1/4 "

1/4" strip

Glue a sheet of tin foil (shiny side up) to a sheet of computer paper. When dry, draw a 4" x 8" rectangle on the paper side and cut out. With a ruler, draw three lines 1/4" apart.

2.

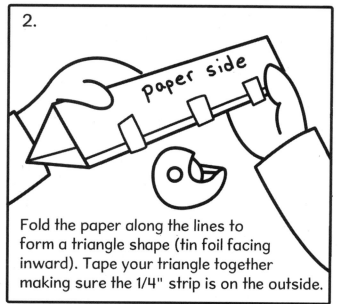

paper side

Fold the paper along the lines to form a triangle shape (tin foil facing inward). Tape your triangle together making sure the 1/4" strip is on the outside.

Use your ruler and cut the paper towel tube so it measures 8" long. Slide tin foil triangle inside tube.

4.

Turn paper towel tube on one end and trace a circle around it on black paper. Cut out the circle and tape it to one end of tube. Use your pencil to poke a hole in the center of the black paper.

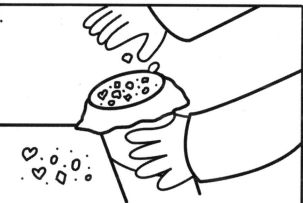

Place a square of plastic wrap on the other end of the tube and press down to make a pouch. Place beads and sequins in pouch. Make sure they have room to move around.

6.

Place a square of wax paper over the pouch of beads and cover with a rubber band. This will hold pouch and wax paper in place. Trim the excess plastic wrap and wax paper.

Let's Make Perfume

Flowers smell nice because of the oils in their petals. The oil dissolves into the rubbing alcohol.

I recycled a baby food jar.

You will need:

lemon peel

flower petals

small jar with lid

rubbing alcohol

Fill your jar with petals. Have an adult pour rubbing alcohol into the jar and seal the lid. After about a week, open the jar and dab a few drops of liquid on your wrist. When dry, smell your wrist. Also try this experiment with lemon or orange peels.

Quicksand

"Quicksand" Recipe:
Mix 1 1/4 cups cornstarch and 1 cup water in a bowl. The mixture should feel like honey and look like heavy cream.

When you've made your quicksand, gently lay your hand on the surface. Notice how your hand sinks into the mixture. Next, try to move your hand through it quickly. Feel how difficult it is to move. This is how real quicksand behaves.

The way liquids move is affected by **viscosity**. Quicksand (and the cornstarch mixture) are **non-Newtonian fluids** which means their **viscosity** changes depending on the pressure applied to it.

When I moved slowly, the quicksand behaved like a liquid. But when I tried to move quickly it behaved like a solid.

Quicksand happens when sand becomes super saturated with water and is often found along beaches, lakes, rivers, marshes and swamps.

cornstarch

water

bowl

spoon

Moldy Pumpkin

This fall, grow mold using your jack-o'-lantern.

Mold is an example of a **fungus**. A fungus is a type of plant that does not produce seeds. It reproduces by releasing **spores** into the air. When the spores land they grow into new **fungi**.

pumpkin

knife

small plastic storage bags

marker

fridge

Have an adult helper cut your pumpkin into pieces that will fit inside a small plastic sto
bag. Close your bag most of the way, leaving a little open to let air in
(mold needs air and moisture to grow). Label each bag by location and place them
in various areas such as your fridge, windowsill, garage etc. Look at your samples
daily and record weekly how much your mold has grown depending on its environment

Moldy Pumpkin Chart

Directions: Under the location column, list areas your pumpkin pieces are placed. You can use the ones listed or add your own. Under the first date, record how much mold has grown on each pumpkin piece. Is there any mold, a few spots, covered?

Beginning date: **Location**	Date:	Date:	Date:	Date:
refrigerator				
windowsill				
closet				
outside				

Rainbow in a Jar

Fill a glass jar with water and set it on the windowsill in bright sunlight. Place a white sheet of paper on the floor in front of the window (the larger the paper the larger the rainbow image). A rainbow will be reflected on the paper. Draw lines to capture your rainbow.

A rainbow is a curved arc of light of many colors. They are caused by the sun shining through drops of water during or after a rain.

The light is separated into seven colors: red, orange, yellow, green, blue, indigo and violet.

crayons

Rainbow Milk

Pour enough milk to cover bottom of plate. Add a drop or two of each color of food coloring into the milk, evenly spaced. Squeeze a little bit of dishwashing liquid into the center of the plate of milk and enjoy the show!

Milk consists of several molecules including fat, proteins and sugars. The detergent reacts with the protein in the milk and alters the shape of the molecules.

Milk is largely made of water and has a **surface tension**. Dish soap is good at destroying surface tension (bonds between the water molecules).

You will need:

dishwashing liquid

2% or whole milk

pie plate or shallow dish

food coloring

Magic Plastic

Plastic containers found at delis, salad bars and grocery stores work well for this project. Cut your plastic container into a flat sheet. Use permanent markers to draw your designs on the plastic. Cut your designs out with scissors and place on a cookie sheet. Have an adult helper place your plastic into a 350 degree oven. Watch for the plastic to shrink (a 5 to 6 inch piece of plastic will take up to 3 1/2 minutes). The plastic will curl then flatten out when it is ready. Have your adult helper remove the plastic and allow to cool before handling.

Shrinking plastic is a great example of how **thermoplastics** are made. Plastics are made of long chainlike molecules called **polymers.** Since polymer chains are so long they can be manipulated to create properties like **polystyrene.** (the #6 plastic like the ones used for grocery store salads).

#6 plastic container

permanent markers

scissors

Plastic containers with this symbol will shrink when heated.

The **polystyrene** (#6 plastic) stays in a stretched state unless something causes it to change. Polystyrene is a thermo-plastic because it goes back to its original state when it is heated.

Rubber Chicken Bone

Make a hard chicken bone feel like it's made of rubber.

The bone becomes rubbery because of the loss of **calcium** in the bone. We need calcium to keep our bones strong.

A clean pickle jar works great for this experiment!

You will need:

white vinegar

- cooked chicken bone

jar with lid

Have an adult remove as much meat from the bone as possible. Place the bone in a jar filled with white vinegar. Place the lid on the jar and leave bone in the vinegar for 7 days. Test the bone daily to check flexibility. By the end of the week, your bone will feel very rubbery!

-Vinegar is an acid that reacts chemically with the bone by removing the calcium compounds in it.

Salt Crystals

In a **crystal**, atoms or molecules join together to form a pattern that repeats itself over and over to create a certain shape.

EPSOM SALT

tin pie plate

spoon

sponge

scissors

food coloring

Have an adult boil a 1/2 cup water in the microwave. Stir 1/4 cup of Epsom salt into the hot water until it is dissolved. Add drops of food coloring if you like. Pour the mixture over a piece of sponge sitting in a shallow pan. Keep pan in a warm, sunny location. Crystals will form as the water evoporates.

pH Indicator

pH stands for, "potential Hydrogen" and measures how much acid or alkali (base) a substance contains.

Red cabbage juice contains a natural pH indicator that changes color depending on the acidity of a solution.

Indicator Chart

pH results

Make a chart to sho
what colors your
solutions changed i

red cabbage (looks purple)

bowl of hot water

glass jar and strainer

coffee fil

scissor

chopping board

"...ed" cabbage ...ntains pigments ...lled **anthocyanins** ...ich gives it the ...rple color.

Your solution will turn red-yellow in acid, green-blue in neutrals and purple blue in alkali based substances.

vinegar

milk

soapy water

plastic containers

...can also ...e pH paper to ...your ...tions. Soak ...ee filters in ...r cabbage juice, ...e to dry and ...into strips.

To make your pH indicator, have an adult chop a head of red cabbage into small pieces. Let it sit in a bowl of hot water for several hours (or you can boil your bowl of water/cabbage in the microwave for about 10 minutes). The darker the water gets, the better the results. When cool, strain water into a glass jar.

In small plastic containers, add a tablespoon of each test substance and label. With a teaspoon, pour a little of your pH indicator into the cups and watch the colors change. Testing solutions: water, milk, sports drink, vinegar, shampoo, baking soda mixed in water.

Snowflake Study

Snowflakes form when water freezes around tiny bits of dust in the air.

Snowflakes are always 6 sided because the atoms in water molecules are arranged in triangles.

The size and shape of a snowflake depends on the temperature, moisture in the air, and how much time it has to grow before hitting the ground.

When the snow starts to fall, bundle up, grab a piece of black paper and a magnifying glass. Catch a couple of snowflakes on your paper and observe them with your magnifier. Compare how your snowflakes are different or the same.

White Light

White light is created when the 7 colors of the rainbow blend together. Your eyes see all the shades but your brain mixes them together which makes it appear white.

string/yarn

ruler

scissors

markers: red, orange, yellow, blue, dark blue, purple, green.

card stock

plastic lid

Use a butter dish lid to trace a circle on a sheet of card stock. Cut out. Draw 6 lines to make 7 equal sections. Color each section with your 7 rainbow colors. Poke 2 holes in the circle 1/2" apart. Push a long piece of string (about 30-36") through the holes and tie into a knot. Hold a loop in each hand and flip your rainbow colored disk around several times to wind the string tightly. Now, pull your hands apart to make the disk spin quickly.

Rock Candy

Mixing water and sugar makes a **super saturated solution**. This mean that the water can only hold the suga when both are really hot.

1 Tie string to the middle of a pencil and attach a paper clip to the other end. The string will act as the **seed** for the crystal.

2 Have an adult bring water to a boil in a pan. Slowly pour sugar into boiling water and stir until all of it is dissolved.

3 After it cools down a little have your adult helper pour the sugar solution into a glass jar.

4 Carefully submerge your string into the jar, making sure it sits in the middle and does not touch the bottom. If it hangs too far, roll the string around the pencil until it's the right length. Rest the pencil on the rim of jar.

5 Leave your rock candy to grow for at least a week. Observe the changes daily.

When the water cools, the sugar comes out of the solution and turns back into sugar crystals on your string.

ou will
eed:

2 cups sugar

glass jar

string

paper clip

1 cup water

pencil

See Sound

Take a sheet of tin foil and wrap it tightly over the top of a plastic butter dish. Sprinkle some salt on top of the tin foil. Hold the can over the salt and tap with a wooden spoon. Explore different ways of holding and tapping the can to get the salt moving.

Sound vibrations travel through the air and when they hit the foil stretched over the can like a drum, it vibrates. Your ear also has a drum (eardrum) and works because of sound vibrations too.

You will need:

empty tin can

wooden spoon

empty plastic butter dish

tin foil ↑

salt

Grow a Stalactite

Fill 2 jars with hot water and mix in as much baking soda as will dissolve. Attach a paper clip to the ends of a long piece of string (or yarn). Place the ends in the jars so the string hangs between the jars. Put a saucer between the jars to catch the drips.

Stalactites form over many centuries as water drips and deposits minerals. But you can make your own in less than a week.

Stalactites are long rock columns that grow from the roof of a cave and hang down.

You will need:

2 paperclips

spoon

Baking Soda

2 jars

string

Rock Scavenger Hunt

Rocks are made of one or more **minerals.** A mineral forms in the earth from matter that was never alive.

There are 3 types of rocks: **igneous, sedimentary** and **metamorphic.**

Igneous- rocks that form from melted materials.
Sedimentary- layers of rock made from shell and other materials that sink to the bottom of lakes and oceans.
Metamorphic- igneous or sedimentary rock whose minerals have been changed by strong heat.

collect, compare and classify.

Rocks
1. smooth
2. black
3. flat
4. sparkles
5. holes
6. gray
7. pink

Use an egg carton to gather and store your rocks.

Volcano Eruption

Eruption

You will need:

red food coloring

plastic bottle

liquid detergent

baking soda

warm water

vinegar

plate

All chemical reactions are about the making or destroying of bonds between atoms in which carbon dioxide gas is made - just like a real volcano.

The gas bubbles build up in the bottle and force the liquid "lava" up and over the mouth of the "volcano."

3. Fill the bottle with warm water almost to the top. Add a few drops of food coloring. Squeeze 6 drops of liquid detergent into bottle. Add 2 tablespoons of baking soda. Slowly pour vinegar into the bottle and watch your volcano erupt!

Wiggly Worms

Tear strands of cooked spaghetti into several worm sized pieces. In a large clear plastic deli cup, mix vinegar with water. Slowly add the baking soda then drop in the pieces of cooked spaghetti. Watch your "worms" come to life.

1 cup white vinegar

2 tablespoons baking soda

1 cup water

You will need:

cooked spaghetti

The noodles sink to the bottom because they are more **dense** (heavier) than water. The bubbles rise because they are **less dense** (lighter) than water.

Wind Energy

Moving air, even someone's breath is considered wind. Explore different wind energies that make your pinwheel spin.

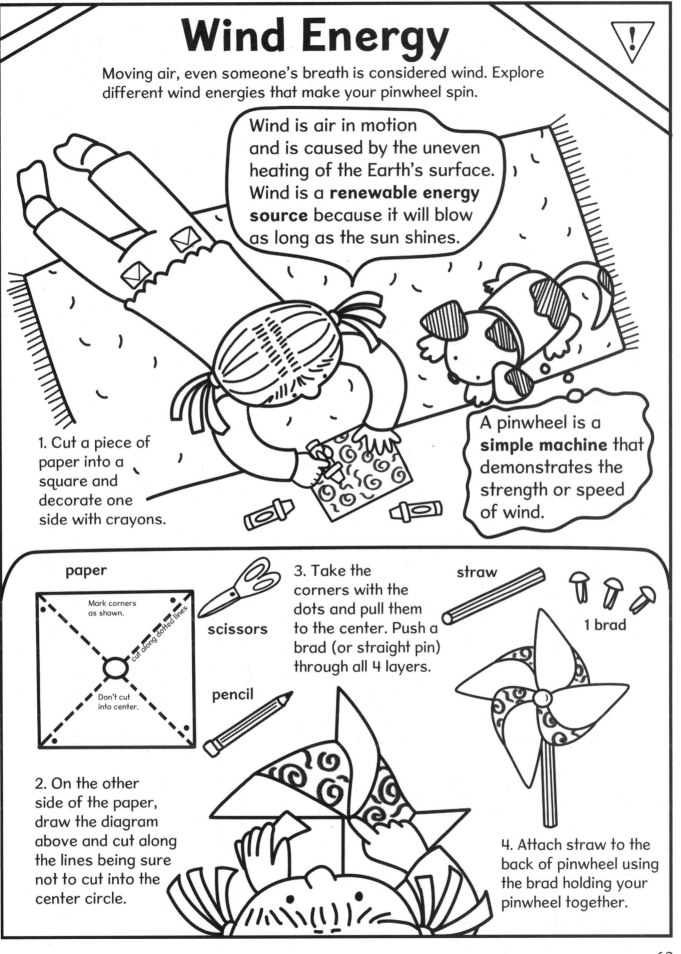

Wind is air in motion and is caused by the uneven heating of the Earth's surface. Wind is a **renewable energy source** because it will blow as long as the sun shines.

A pinwheel is a **simple machine** that demonstrates the strength or speed of wind.

1. Cut a piece of paper into a square and decorate one side with crayons.

paper

Mark corners as shown.

cut along dotted lines

Don't cut into center.

scissors

pencil

3. Take the corners with the dots and pull them to the center. Push a brad (or straight pin) through all 4 layers.

straw

1 brad

2. On the other side of the paper, draw the diagram above and cut along the lines being sure not to cut into the center circle.

4. Attach straw to the back of pinwheel using the brad holding your pinwheel together.

Seedy Socks

This project works best in late summer and into fall.

Find an old sock and fit it over your shoe. Wander around outside wherever plants and weeds are growing. Carefully remove your sock and observe the tiny seeds you've picked up. Set aside. Line a shoebox with a plastic garbage bag and fill with potting soil. Take your seedy sock and cut a portion that has the most seeds attached. Lay it on the soil, seeds facing up, and cover with a layer of soil. Water your seeds. Your seedlings will begin sprouting within the week. What did you grow?

"Hitchhikers" are seeds that have tiny hooks that grab onto fur from passing animals or on people's clothing. Hitchhikers inspired the invention of the fabric hook-and-loop fastener.

Birds often eat berries which contain seeds. The seeds are not digested, instead they are in the birds poop. The poop lands somewhere else and the seed is **dispersed**.

Seeds travel by sailing on the wind, floating on the water or on animals. Seed travel is called **dissemination**.

plastic bag

potting soil

old sock

water

shoebox

scissors

Soap Study

Fill 2 glass jars half way with water. Add a drop of food coloring to each. Add 1/4 cup of cooking oil to each jar. Add a few squirts of liquid soap to one of the jars. Screw th lids on both jars and shake the jars vigorously for 30 seconds to mix the contents. Le both jars to settle, compare the contents in both. What happened to the jar with the so liquid included?

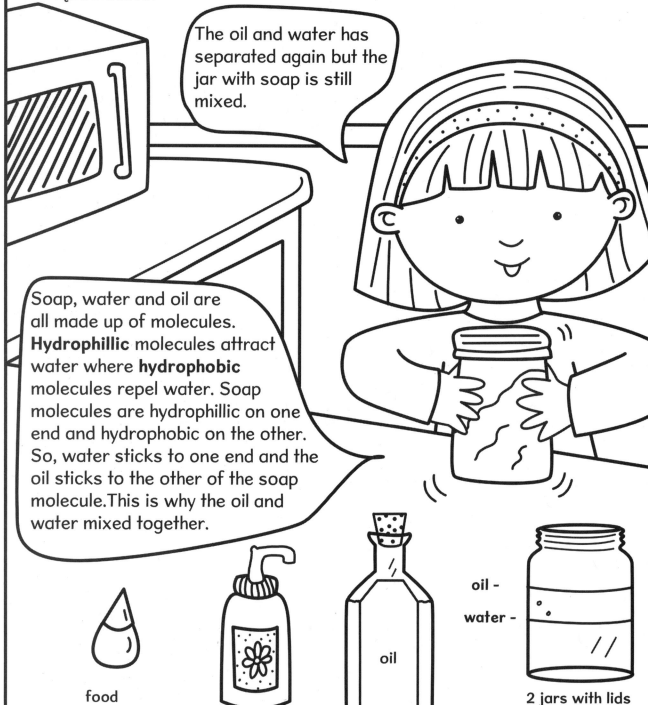

The oil and water has separated again but the jar with soap is still mixed.

Soap, water and oil are all made up of molecules. **Hydrophillic** molecules attract water where **hydrophobic** molecules repel water. Soap molecules are hydrophillic on one end and hydrophobic on the other. So, water sticks to one end and the oil sticks to the other of the soap molecule. This is why the oil and water mixed together.

food coloring

liquid soap

oil

oil -

water -

2 jars with lids

Recycled Soap

Save old, tiny slivers of left over soap and keep them in a plastic travel soap container. When your container is full, have an adult help you melt them using a glass measuring cup. Microwave on high for 30 seconds. Stir. Continue melting 15 seconds at a time (stir between sets) until melted. Pour your soapy soup into your travel soap container (or a decorative mold). Allow soap to cool and harden. Enjoy your new bar of soap!

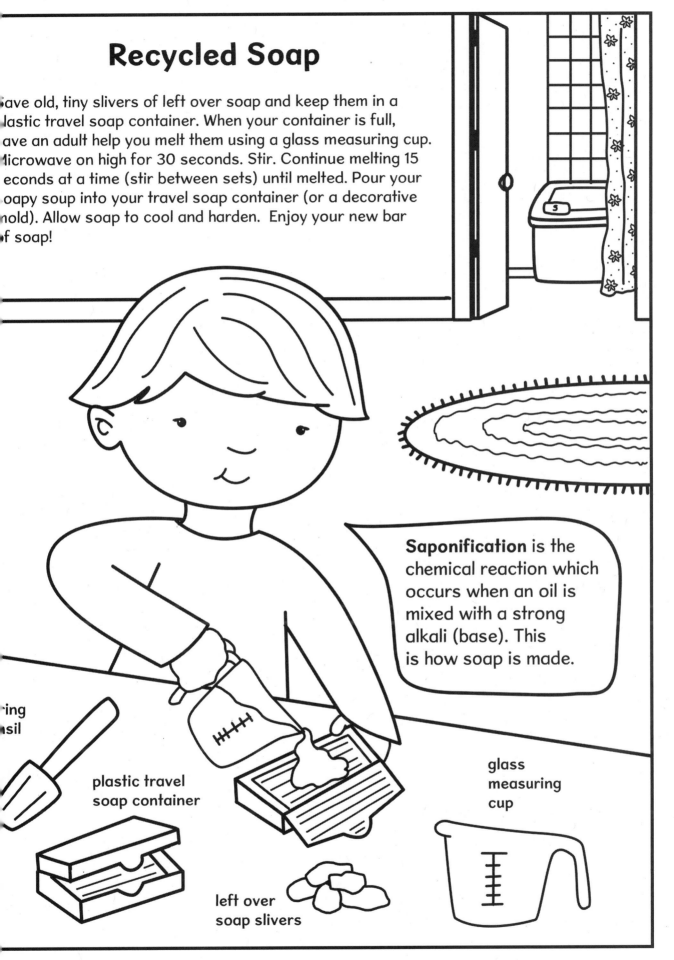

Saponification is the chemical reaction which occurs when an oil is mixed with a strong alkali (base). This is how soap is made.

ring
sil

plastic travel soap container

left over soap slivers

glass measuring cup

String Telephone

Use a pencil to poke a small hole in the bottom of the paper cups. Thread the ends of a long piece of string through the holes of each cup. Knot the ends and attach a paper clip to keep it from pulling through the holes. Have your friend hold one cup while you walk far enough away to make the string tight (the string has to be tight or it won't work). Take turns speaking and listening.

When you talk into the cup, it vibrates back and forth with **sound waves**. The vibration travels through the string and into the second cup. The second person can hear the sound waves.

You will need:

2 paper clips

2 paper cups

pencil

string

Test Your Taste Buds

When we eat, we smell and taste the food at the same time because our nose shares the same airway as our mouth.

Blindfold your test subject, making sure they don't see the food they'll be tasting. Select a variety of sweet, salty, sour and bitter flavored foods for the taste test. Place food in containers (fast food dip containers work well).

Round one: Place one item at a time on the subject's tongue and have them guess what they are eating. Document results.

Round two: Have the subject plug their nose and eat the same foods again. Compare results. Did their sense of smell affect their answers?

Taste Receptors
bitter
sour
salty
sweet

Our tongues are covered in tiny bumps called **papillae** and contain our taste buds.

Suggestions: sugar cubes, salt, fruits, vegetables, vinegar.

Confused taste buds:
Hold an onion under test subject's nose and have them breathe deeply. Feed them a piece of apple and ask them what they are eating. Did they think they ate a piece of onion?

Whale Blubber

With a spatula, smear some lard in the first baggy. Place your hand in the baggy making sure your hand is covered in the lard. Place your other hand (or have a friend participate) in the second baggy without lard. Place both hands in the ice water. Which hand can you keep in the ice water longer?

Blubber is a fatty tissue found under the skin of whales and other warm blooded mammals. It acts as an **insulator** by keeping their temperature at 95 degrees even in very cold water.

The blubber also stores nutrients that their body can use when they are in waters where there isn't much food.

bowl of ice and water

You will need:

2 plastic storage bags

lard

spatula

Bubble Fun

bubble recipe:

1/2 cup dishwashing liquid

2 cups water

2 teaspoons sugar

A dab of food coloring (optional)

Mix and pour in a shallow pan.

Bubbles are bits of air or gas trapped inside a liquid sphere. Anything wet can enter the bubble without breaking it because the wet surface meeting the soapy film becomes part of it.

Turn a plastic cup upside down and wet bottom of cup with the bubble mixture. Use a bubble wand (or pipe cleaner shaped into a wand) to blow a large bubble on top of the cup. Wet straw in bubble mix and gently push it through the bubble. Blow a smaller bubble inside the large one.

You will need:

straws

plastic cup

bubble wand

bubble mix

Make a Wormery

Earthworms are very important for the soil. They enjoy eating decaying matter and their waste (poop) is high in nitrate, potash, phosphorus and magnesium. These are all essential for a plant's growth.

1. Find 2 to 3 earthworms in the garden. The best time to find them is after a good rain.

earthworms

masking tape

chopped onion and potato

sand

shoebox

large plastic bottle

sharp pencil

scissors

dry leaves

damp soil

3. Have an adult helper cut the top of a plastic bottle so it will fit inside the upright shoe box. Also ask them to chop some onion and potato chunks for your wormery.

2. Tape one side of the shoebox lid to the shoebox so it opens like a door. Poke air holes to the top of the box with a pencil.

4. Fill your bottle with layers of sand, soil, sand, soil. Top with chopped onion and potato. Add some dry leaves. Place your worms in the bottle and fit into the shoebox. Close the lid and put the worms in a cool, dry location.

Worms dig and **"tunnel,"** which moves nutrients and air from the ground level to the soil.

before

after

5. After 4 days, open the shoebox and observe the changes to the soil. Release your worms back to the garden.

Windsocks

Remove lid and have an adult help cut the bottom out of the ice cream tub. Decorate your container with craft supplies (construction paper, markers, stickers, paint, etc). Tape long strips of crepe paper to the bottom inside of the ice cream container. Let dry. Punch 4 hole at the top of the tub evenly spaced. Threa 4 long pieces of string through holes and knot together. Tie another long string to the knot to hang your windsock.

Windsocks are found at airports and sometimes near highways in windy locations.

A windsock is used to show wind direction and **relative wind speed.**

You will need:

crepe paper

1/2 gallon ice cream tub

construction paper

poster paint

markers

tape

string/yarn

74

Windsock #2

Have an adult help you cut the top and bottom off of a plastic soda bottle (use the lines where the label once laid as a guide). Punch 2 holes at the top of the bottle about 1/2" from the top, equally on opposite sides. On the bottom, punch holes evenly spaced all the way around (about 15 holes). Use scraps of ribbon (the same length) and thread each through the holes at the bottom and tie with a knot. Take another strip of ribbon, thread through the top two holes and tie into a knot. Attach a long piece of string to the knot to hang your windsock.

#2

Windspeed is shown by the windsock's angle. In low winds, it droops. In high winds it flies horizontally. Wind direction is the opposite direction of the direction the windsock is pointing.

— cut

— cut

scissors

hole punch

ribbon scraps

soda bottle